A Mother's Bouquet
Rosary Meditations
For Moms

Sherry Boas

Caritas Press, USA

A MOTHER'S BOUQUET
Rosary Meditations for Moms

Sherry Boas

Second Edition

10 9 8 7 6 5 4 3 2

ISBN 978-098338663-6

For reorders, visit LilyTrilogy.com or
CatholicWord.com

Published by Caritas Press, Arizona, USA

INTRODUCTION

Why should busy moms pray the rosary? St. Louis de Montfort said that praying the rosary devoutly dons Jesus and Mary with crowns of red and white roses that never fade or whither. The word rosary means "crown of roses." Some people say they have even smelled the sweet aroma of roses while praying the rosary. Such is the power of these prayers to pierce the floor of Heaven and allow a portion of Paradise to seep through.

The Rosary is something any mother can devote herself to. It can fit into any schedule. Unlike so many other commitments, it does not have to be done at a particular time, in a specific place. It does not even have to be prayed on beads, if our hands are busy tending to the needs of the precious little ones God has entrusted to us. I have recited my Rosary on the fingers of my newborn babies as I rocked them to sleep. I have recited it in the back yard, gathering ten rocks and giving them to my toddler to put in a flower pot after each Hail Mary. Of course, the beauty of the Rosary becomes particularly clear to us busy moms when we find a place of quiet solitude and a solid block of time to meditate on the mysteries – especially if we are fortunate enough to be able to pray in the presence of Jesus in the Blessed Sacrament. But even the family room can be a sanctuary if, while the kids are tucked in bed, we spend even fifteen minutes with our Lord and our Lady.

You can quiet your mind, heart and soul, breathing in the Holy Spirit, as you let the Rosary beads pass one by one through your fingers. What a gift of renewal bestowed on us by our Blessed Mother, who knows better than any other human being, the challenges, sufferings, sacrifices, rewards and blessings of the holy vocation of motherhood. Our Lady asks everyone to pray the Rosary every day to combat the evils of this world. No one is more concerned about the future than us mothers. Mary tells us, in her Church-approved apparitions, that we can change the future by praying the Rosary. It is a way for us to leave our children a better world.

The Rosary also procures more immediate benefits for our children. If we pray the Rosary faithfully and strive to live what we have learned, we will become imitators of Mary, the perfect mother. We will grow to love her Son more, and loving Him means loving everyone God places in our lives, especially the children.

The meditations in this book are meant to help you grow in devotion to Jesus, the Blessed Virgin Mary, your family and all the children of the world. May the spiritual bouquets created by your rosaries bring the fragrance of heaven into your heart and home. And may your children and all future generations be blessed by the abiding blooms.

THE
JOYFUL
MYSTERIES

I

THE ANNUNCIATION

"May it be done to me."   *Luke 1:38*

Jesus, I remember the moment I learned I was to become a mother. My heart was full of joy and hope and anticipation of the wondrous miracle that was taking place. And yet, that joy is too often lost in the day-to-day duties of motherhood, and I take for granted the beautiful treasure that you've entrusted to me. If I allow strife and stress to destroy my peace, it is because I am not abandoned to your will, not willing to sacrifice and suffer, not willing to let go of my selfish designs for my day or my hour or my moment. If the privilege of serving these precious ones becomes drudgery, it is because I fail to surrender my every moment to you. Lord, help me proclaim, with every beating of my heart, Mary's fiat when the angel Gabriel announced to her that she would bear the Savior. "Behold I am the handmaid of the Lord. May it be done to me according to your word."

II

THE VISITATION

"At the moment the sound of your greeting reached my ears, the infant in my womb leaped for joy."

Luke 1:44

An unborn child, John the Baptist, was the first to proclaim the coming of the Savior of the world. This says something profound, Lord, about the helpless innocence you have given to my care. All too often, I forget that your Kingdom belongs to the children and those who become like them. Give me a deep awe and respect for the precious ones you have entrusted to me. Help me understand what a supreme honor it is to see the world through their simple eyes, especially things of the Spirit. Help me to learn from them as I teach them your love. And help me each day to become more like my humble Mother Mary, who fully understood the immeasurable honor of being a mother and who, upon learning of her role in life, told her cousin Elizabeth, "The Mighty One has done great things for me."

III

THE NATIVITY

"You will find an infant wrapped in swaddling clothes and lying in a manger."

Luke 2:12

Lord, let me have a taste of Mary's awe, as she gazed into your face -- Almighty God, so helpless and dependent upon her. Help me see in the face of every baby the lesson of the Nativity – that humility and simplicity ushered the Christ child into the world. The most important birth ever was the most humble. The most exalted was the lowliest. Jesus, you are far above all, yet you were born in a stable – an unfit place for any newborn, and most especially the Savior of the world.

I remember how I prepared for my children in every way possible, knowing my baby deserves the best I can provide. An expectant mother buys clothing and blankets, paints the nursery, chooses the crib ever so carefully, making sure it is a safe, warm and comfortable place to lay her precious little one. Yet Mary had no nursery and no crib – no place but an animal's trough to lay her baby boy.

Your choice, Heavenly Father, to bring your Son, my Savior, into the world in such a humble place gives me great hope. When I ask you, Jesus, to come into my heart, I know it is just as unfit as that stable in Bethlehem. It is not the palace a king deserves. Yet, you love me so much, you are willing to come in and make it ever more holy with each beat. What was once mere shelter for ox and lambs is now holy ground. So my heart is transformed because you live there.

IV

THE PRESENTATION

"They took him up to Jerusalem to present him to the Lord."

Luke 2:22

Lord, I present all my children to you. They are this life's greatest blessings, but I do not own them. No soul is any other's possession. Every human being belongs to you. My children are on loan to me, sent into this family for the fulfillment of your perfect plan of love and redemption. May I do my part to fashion them into faithful disciples who will serve you well as members of the Body of Christ.

Just as Mary and Joseph consecrated baby Jesus to you, I long to consecrate my children, setting them apart for your service. May these tiny hands I hold do your work some day in building up the kingdom. May these tiny feet I wash carry the Good News someday into an aching world. May the faces I kiss always reflect your love to all who gaze upon them. May I never forget the unfathomable privilege you have given me – that of helping you shape souls that will love and praise you forever.

V

FINDING JESUS IN THE TEMPLE

"When his parents saw him, they were astonished, and his mother said to him, "Son, why have you done this to us? Your father and I have been looking for you with great anxiety." And he said to them, "Why were you looking for me? Did you not know that I must be in my Father's House?"

Luke 2:48-49

Lord Jesus, as Mary found you in the Temple, help me find you in my home each day. Let me find you in my husband and children, created in your image. Give me a deep devotion to you as the Christ Child, so I might see you in everyone who is vulnerable, especially the dear children you have entrusted to me.

I cannot even fathom the joy of putting my arms around you as a little boy, Jesus. Yet, when I hold my children, I do hold you. You said of the little ones, "Whoever receives one child such as this in my name, receives me." I need look no farther than home to find you, Jesus. You are in the laughter of tiny voices, the tears on chubby cheeks. You are in the piles of laundry and stacks of dirty dishes, because you said, "What you do to the least of these, you do to me."

The duties I perform, I do for love of my family – and for love of you, because you have trusted me with this work. You have chosen me to serve these precious souls, united as family. Your assignment of these duties gives my work its dignity. I pour my love into accomplishing it, and in that love, I find you.

THE
LUMINOUS
MYSTERIES

I

THE BAPTISM OF JESUS

"After Jesus was baptized, he came up from the water and behold, the heavens were opened for him, and he saw the Spirit of God descending like a dove and coming upon him."

Matthew 3:16

The miracle of my children's birth is utterly breathtaking. And yet, equally as miraculous is their rebirth into the family of God through the Sacrament of Baptism. I am so grateful to you, Lord Jesus, for allowing my children to share in your baptism, to share in your very life. It is my duty and my profound privilege to bring my children to you, since it is you who have given them to me.

May I never cease to marvel at my good fortune, to spend my days and nights with sinless creatures – pure and holy souls who have not been in this world long enough to know serious sin and whose original sin has been washed away in the waters of baptism. May I never fail to see your grace shining in their faces – the grace that makes their souls bright and beautiful and bound for Heaven.

II

THE WEDDING FEAST AT CANA

"When the wine ran short, the mother of Jesus said to him, 'They have no wine.' And Jesus said to her, 'Woman, how does your concern affect me? My hour has not yet come.' His mother said to the servers, 'Do whatever he tells you.'"

John 2:3-5

Lord, the very first miracle you ever performed publicly was at a wedding. Why did you choose to manifest your divinity for the first time and launch your public ministry at a wedding? This tells us a great deal about God's view of marriage. It is the sacrament of marriage that brings children into the world and into God's family. To know that God places such great value on families, bound together by sacrament and love, is to know the honor attached to my role as mother. My calling is to live up to that honor through self sacrifice and charity.

The wedding at Cana also tells us something else about how God views motherhood. Jesus performed the miracle – turning the water into wine – at the request of his mother, even though he had just said, " My hour has not yet come." Jesus is moved to action by Mary's gentle persistence and deep act of faith, as she tells the waiters "Do whatever he tells you."

III

THE PROCLAMATION OF THE KINGDOM

"After John had been arrested, Jesus came to Galilee proclaiming the gospel of God: 'This is the time of fulfillment. The kingdom of God is at hand. Repent, and believe in the gospel.'"

Mark 1:14-15

Lord, I know there is no more important work I have as a parent than proclaiming your kingdom to my children, teaching them your love, your mercy, your commands, showing them the wonders of the world you created. Part of that teaching consists in telling them, day by day, of the mysteries of the faith, centering the life of our family around the Church, incorporating the language of Heaven into our daily vocabulary, praying in the morning, at night and at meal times, thanking you whenever we receive blessings, petitioning when we have worries, praising you always.

But proclaiming the kingdom also requires preaching without words. It requires teaching by example the beauty of your kingdom, creating in our home a sanctuary of love, respect and forgiveness that speak to their hearts about your goodness.

Much of what my children believe about me, they will believe about you, Lord. They will view you as the kind of parent I am. Help me be a worthy image of you -- a reflection of your perfect love, so that my children will never want to stray from your embrace and so they might spend their lives proclaiming your gospel of love.

IV

THE TRANSFIGURATION

"Lord, it is good that we are here."

Mark 17:4

Lord Jesus, you took Peter, John and James to the top of a mountain to pray. While you were praying, your face shone like the sun and your clothes became dazzling white. Moses and Elijah appeared, and you spoke with them. No doubt, your disciples did not want this glorious sight to end. So Peter said, "Lord, it is good that we are here; if you wish, I will make three tents here, one for you, one for Moses and one for Elijah."

Dear Lord, how I understand Peter. How often I have wanted to be apart with you on the mountain, but just as Peter, John and James had to come back down the mountain for the work that was ahead of them, so I too must depart from my place of peace and prayer to serve the souls you have placed in my care. The disciples got a taste of Heaven by witnessing the Transfiguration, but they had much work and much suffering in front of them before they would dine at the Heavenly banquet prepared for them in Paradise.

The moments when I rest in your presence, Lord, are foreshadows of a place I hope to reach when this life's pilgrimage is through. But my quiet times of contemplation or glorious times of worship must be interrupted, oftentimes by not so peaceful events -- bickering children, babies with colic, ringing phones, blenders and mixers, traffic jams and TVs. But I am not unlike the disciples. They walked down the mountain right into a big crowd, where scribes were arguing with the rest of your disciples. And the father of a boy who was in convulsions pleaded with you to drive out the evil spirit.

How much nicer it would have been to stay on the mountain. But love called you and your disciples back down. You knew there were people who needed you. Love calls me down too.

V

THE INSTITUTION OF
THE HOLY EUCHARIST

"Jesus took bread, said the blessing, broke it and giving it to his disciples said, 'Take and eat. This is my body.' Then he took a cup, gave thanks and gave it to them, saying, 'drink from it, all of you, for this is my blood of the Covenant, which will be shed on behalf of many for the forgiveness of sins.'"

Matthew 26:26-27

Each one of us is called to be Eucharist -- broken and shared, poured out for one another. Mothers, especially, have this privilege of making a life-giving sacrifice for their children. We give our children our very selves -- not just everything we *have*, but everything we *are*. We would give our flesh and our last drop of blood for them. The pelican has long been a symbol of Christ in the Blessed the Sacrament. The mother bird will press her beak into her chest and feed her young on her own blood rather than let them starve. This is what motherhood is – a minute by minute act of total self–giving, a complete pouring out of self for the other.

I thank you, Lord, for your perfect and holy sacrifice, for giving me your body and blood, so I might be strengthened for the demands of my vocation. I unite all my sacrifices, my sufferings, my trials, Lord Jesus, with the Holy Sacrifice of the Mass, so that my offering to the Heavenly Father may be made perfect through you. And I beg you to pour your grace into my soul each time I receive Holy Communion, so I may become the self-giving mother you have called me to be.

THE

SORROWFUL

MYSTERIES

I

AGONY IN THE GARDEN

"Not my will, but yours be done."
Luke 22:42

What a beautiful journey to holiness you have chosen for me, God, when you gave me the vocation of motherhood. Holiness requires surrendering one's will completely to you. There is perhaps no better way to learn this than through motherhood. It is a calling that requires me, at every moment, to subordinate my own needs to the needs of my family. How simple, and yet how difficult for us humans. But it is painless compared to the suffering that you accepted when, in the garden, you told your father, "not my will, but yours be done." For the most part, my day-to-day sacrifice is not agony, it is simply inconvenience or frustration. And then, every once in a while, true agony does enter in, and I must learn to offer it up to you, Lord, and allow you to use it for the salvation of souls. It is at these moments, and all moments, indeed, that I am called to die to myself and live in your most holy will.

II

THE SCOURGING AT THE PILLAR

"By His stripes we were healed."
Isaiah 53:5

Lord, help me accept without complaint the physical difficulties of motherhood, be it the pains of labor and delivery, exhaustion due to sleep deprivation or the fatigue of carrying heavy groceries and growing children. Help me to remember that love is sacrifice. Only suffering earns us the right to call it love. May I embrace my sufferings for the welfare of my family as you, Jesus, embraced your sufferings for the salvation of the world.

The prophet Isaiah tells us that upon you "was the chastisement that makes us whole" and that by your "stripes we were healed." Too often, I hear myself complaining about the smallest of inconveniences, forgetting how much you, Lord, had to bear for my sake. Though you were harshly treated, you submitted and opened not your mouth; like a lamb led to the slaughter, you were silent. Help me, Lord, to be more like you and accept my sufferings – large and small – in silent submission to your most holy will.

III

THE CROWNING WITH THORNS

"Weaving a crown of thorns, they placed it on his head and a reed in his right hand. And kneeling before him, they mocked Him, saying, 'Hail, King of the Jews!' They spat upon Him..."
Matthew 27:29-30

Motherhood is a woman's crowning glory, but the world mocks it, just as it mocked you, Jesus, giving you a crown of thorns in lieu of a crown of gold. The world ridicules sacrifice and self-giving. When it looks at a mother's hands, it sees demanding work rather than labor of love. When it looks at her worth, it sees a lack of accomplishments rather than an ascent to holiness through self-sacrifice. When it looks at what surrounds her, it sees messy rooms and dirty diapers rather than the arms of pure and innocent souls wrapped around her neck.

Everywhere in our society, we hear voices that decry the duties of parenthood. Everywhere we look, we see people preventing children from coming into their lives. Children are viewed as burdens instead of blessings. Mothers who devote their lives to children, then, are ridiculed, pitied and unappreciated.

Let none of this dismay me, Lord, for I have it from your own lips that this is all part of true discipleship. "The world hated them, because they do not belong to the world, any more than I belong to the world." (John 17:14) The world hates what it sees in motherhood because it cannot penetrate the depths of God's mysteries. I refuse to belong to a world whose eyes cannot look inside a mother's heart and see the unequaled beauty of the treasured little ones concealed within it.

IV

THE CARRYING OF THE CROSS

"As they were going out, they met a Cyrenian named Simon; this man they pressed into service to carry the cross."

Matthew 27:32

Help me, Lord, to persevere in carrying whatever crosses you present to me through this holy vocation of motherhood. The trials of this calling can be many, but it is all for the best cause – preparing the souls you have entrusted to me for sainthood. Give me patience to bear whatever burdens and trials you deem necessary for the salvation of souls. Only through this patience in the face of adversity can I prove my love for you. Only through my perfect surrender will I achieve perfection. As Saint Peter observed, "If you are patient when you suffer for doing what is good, this is a grace before God."

May I not only accept my sufferings as a means to sanctify me, Lord, but may I unite them with Christ's perfect sacrifice and offer them to you for the salvation of my family, whom you and I love so much.

V

THE CRUCIFIXION

"The earth quaked, rocks were split, tombs were opened and the bodies of many saints who had fallen asleep were raised."
Matthew 27:51-52

The Lord of the Universe, the perfect and holy one, hanging on the cross for our sins. How can a human heart begin to comprehend this kind of love? The only hope I have of even partly understanding is in considering my love for my children. Though my love is imperfect and cannot be compared to yours, Jesus, I can well understand how you can love someone else more than yourself, to the point of emptying out everything you have and everything you are.

It is this love for my children that makes me love you, Jesus, all the more. You, indeed, are Savior of my soul, but beyond that, you are Savior of my children's souls. In Acts 2:39, Peter tells the crowd about the gift that you, Jesus, have given the world. "For the promise is made to you and to your children and to all those far off, whomever the Lord our God will call." It is one thing to be grateful for the sacrifice you made to lead *me* to Heaven. But infinitely more grateful is my soul when it remembers that you also suffered and died for my children so *they* could have eternal life. I am in even greater debt to you, Jesus, since I became a mother.

THE
GLORIOUS
MYSTERIES

I

THE RESURRECTION

"Do not let your hearts be troubled ... In my father's house there are many dwelling places. If there were not, would I have told you that I am going to prepare a place for you? And if I go and prepare a place for you, I will come back again and take you to myself, so that where I am you also may be."

John 14: 1-3

After your resurrection, Lord Jesus, you appeared to the Apostles and said, "Peace be with you." How often in my day as a busy mother I need to hear those words from you. If only I could keep them rooted in my heart, so nothing could disturb the peace you give.

So many moments, so many days, I live my life as if the resurrection never happened. I let myself be troubled over the worries of life and even flustered over the most trivial occurrences. If only I could stay focused on what really matters – an eternity with you and my loved ones, won for us by your death and resurrection. This is the reality that calls me to live my life for you –

and for those you have entrusted to my care. This is the reality around which our lives should revolve.

II

THE ASCENSION

"As he blessed them, he parted from them and was taken up to heaven."

Luke 24:51

I can't imagine how our dear Mother Mary must have felt upon seeing her only Son leave this earth in such splendor and glory. Any mother would rejoice to know her child is in the company of the saints and angels, in a place where there is only joy, in union with God, for eternity. And yet, it required of Mary yet another "letting go." She would spend the rest of her years on earth without her perfect son.

As a mother presses her newborn baby to her heart, she has the illusion that the little bundle belongs to her. It fits so perfectly in her arms, rests so sweetly in her embrace. And yet, no soul belongs to another. All souls belong to God. So we must spend our entire lives letting go of our children as they grow more independent throughout the years. Some departures are gradual, some sudden, but eventually separations must come with everything of this life. May I learn to accept them all with the grace that Mary did, and if I can't have my children in my embrace, may I feel blessed to keep them in my heart, understanding that they were never my possession.

III

THE DESCENT OF THE HOLY SPIRIT

"If you love me, you will keep my commandments. And I will ask the Father, and He will give you another advocate to be with you always, the Spirit of truth, which the world cannot accept, because it neither sees nor knows it. But you know it, because it remains with you, and will be in you. I will not leave you orphans; I will come to you."

John 14:15-17

Sometimes as a mother I feel I am tested to my limits. But you promised, Jesus, you would not leave us orphans, that you would send your Spirit to fortify and guide us. I know that I cannot rise to the demands of my calling without the gifts of the Holy Spirit.

I need to call upon these gifts each moment of the day, Lord, if I am to be a mother who demonstrates your love. I need wisdom, understanding, counsel, fortitude, knowledge, piety and fear of the Lord. Help me spend my days and years in pursuit of them, so I can each day become a better mother. I beg you, Lord, for these gifts, for the good of my children. I beg the Holy Spirit to bear fruit in my life, so I may ever grow in love, joy, peace, patience, kindness generosity, faithfulness, gentleness and self-control. I know my children are watching me, and they deserve to witness these virtues, so they can learn how to practice them as well.

IV

THE ASSUMPTION

"Therefore my heart is glad and my soul rejoices, my body, too, abides in confidence; Because you will not abandon my soul to the nether world, nor will you suffer your faithful one to undergo corruption."

Psalms 16:9-10

So much did you love Mary, Lord, that you couldn't let her body know decay. To her belonged the womb that bore you, the hands that rocked you, the lips that kissed you, the feet that followed you to Calvary, the arms that held your lifeless body, taken from the cross.

It is in this kind of pouring out of myself that you sanctity my hands, my lips, my feet, my arms in the daily work you have given me. These are the instruments of your love. They are parts of this mother's body, whose privilege it is to serve the children made in your very image. You see yourself in each one of them, which is why you told us that what we do for the "least" of our brothers, we do for you.

Could it be that Mary is not the only mother who got to hold you and kiss your sweet cheek? Could it be I have this unfathomable opportunity each time I take my children in my arms? How blessed am I to have a body designed to care for and love your precious ones, and in turn, love you. How blessed is the flesh to be imbued with such dignity.

V

THE CORONATION

"A great sign appeared in the sky, a woman clothed with the sun, with the moon under her feet, and on her head a crown of twelve stars."

Revelations 12:1

Sweet Mother Mary, the world tells us that we must fulfill our own needs before considering anyone else's. But your life teaches me something far different. You are first among women, but all your life, you put yourself last. You are Queen of Heaven, but you spent your life as a perfect servant. All generations call you blessed, but you lived in humility and obscurity.

How appropriate that we should call you "blessed." You so perfectly lived the beatitudes.

"Blessed are the poor in spirit, for theirs is the kingdom of heaven." Mary, your poverty of spirit – your "let it be done to me" – won you the crown in Heaven.

"Blessed are the meek, for they will inherit the land." You, Mary have inherited the Church, which calls you Mother, and all the faithful are your spiritual children.

"Blessed are the pure of heart, for they will see God." Mary, you not only saw God, you held him in your arms.

"Blessed are the peacemakers, they will be called children of God." Mary, you so perfectly kept the peace of Christ, through such turmoil and so many trials, that you are called, not only a child of God, but Mother of God and Queen of Peace.

May I too be poor in spirit, meek, pure of heart and a seeker of peace in my family and in this world. May I strive to live these and all the beatitudes in the same spirit you did, Mary, my queen and Mother, so I may love your Son and his kingdom with a heart like yours.

HOW TO PRAY THE ROSARY

1. While holding the crucifix, make the SIGN OF THE CROSS: "In the name of the Father, and of the Son and of the Holy Spirit. Amen."

2. Then, recite the APOSTLE'S CREED:
"I BELIEVE IN GOD, the Father almighty, Creator of heaven and earth, and in Jesus Christ, his only Son, our Lord, who was conceived by the Holy Spirit, born of the Virgin Mary, suffered under Pontius Pilate, was crucified, died and was buried; he descended into hell; on the third day he rose again from the dead; he ascended into heaven, and is seated at the right hand of God the Father almighty; from there he will come to judge the living and the dead. I believe in the Holy Spirit, the holy catholic Church, the communion of saints, the forgiveness of sins, the resurrection of the body, and life everlasting. Amen."

3. Recite the OUR FATHER on the first large Bead:
"OUR FATHER, Who art in heaven, Hallowed be Thy Name. Thy Kingdom come. Thy Will be done, on earth as it is in Heaven. Give us this day our daily bread. And forgive us our trespasses, as we forgive

those who trespass against us. And lead us not into temptation, but deliver us from evil. Amen."

4. On each of the three small beads, recite a HAIL MARY for the increase of faith, hope and love. "HAIL MARY, full of grace, the Lord is with thee; Blessed art thou among women, and blessed is the fruit of thy womb, Jesus. Holy Mary, Mother of God, pray for us sinners, now and at the hour of death. Amen."

5. Recite the GLORY BE on the next large bead.
"GLORY BE to the Father, and to the Son, and to the Holy Spirit. As it was in the beginning, is now, and ever shall be, world without end. Amen."

6. Recall the first Rosary Mystery and recite the Our Father on the next large bead.

7. On each of the adjacent ten small beads (known as a decade), recite a Hail Mary while reflecting on the mystery.

8. On the next large bead, recite the Glory Be.

9. The FATIMA PRAYER may be said here:

"O MY JESUS, forgive us our sins, save us from the fires of hell, lead all souls to heaven, especially those who are in most need of Thy mercy."

10. Begin the next decade by recalling the next mystery and reciting an Our Father. Move to the small beads and pray 10 Hail Marys while meditating on the mystery.

11. Continue until you have circled the entire Rosary (five decades.) Or for a full Rosary, you will circle it four times (twenty decades.)

12. It is customary to CONCLUDE with the following prayers:

HAIL HOLY QUEEN

"HAIL, HOLY QUEEN, mother of mercy, our life, our sweetness, and our hope. To thee do we cry, poor banished children of Eve. To thee do we send up our sighs, mourning and weeping in this valley of tears. Turn then, most gracious advocate, thine eyes of mercy toward us, and after this our exile, show us the blessed fruit of thy womb, Jesus. O clement, O loving, O sweet Virgin Mary.
(Verse) Pray for us, O Holy Mother of God.

(Response) That we may be made worthy of the promises of Christ."

ROSARY PRAYER

(Verse) Let us pray,
(Response) O God, whose only begotten Son, by His life, death, and resurrection, has purchased for us the rewards of eternal salvation, grant, we beseech Thee, that while meditating on these mysteries of the most holy Rosary of the Blessed Virgin Mary, that we may both imitate what they contain and obtain what they promise, through Christ our Lord. Amen.

Most Sacred Heart of Jesus, have mercy on us.

Immaculate Heart of Mary, pray for us.

In the Name of the Father, and of the Son and of the Holy Spirit. Amen.

A NOTE FROM THE AUTHOR

Perhaps if we could see through the eyes of Heaven. Changing a diaper would look sublime. Burping a baby, transcendent. Taking a wiggly toddler to Mass, ethereal.

I think I once got a glimpse of what the angels see.

Our fourth adopted baby had just had his intestine repaired and was faced with the daunting task of learning how to eat from a bottle. John Anthony was born fifteen weeks early, at only a pound and a half, so learning to multitask — simultaneously suck, breathe and swallow — was not easy. It's such a laborious endeavor, that preemies have a tendency to burn more calories than they ingest during any given feeding. I used to pray a rosary on the way to the hospital to give him his bottle. I prayed he would eat. And he did. He ate a little more each day, starting with a nipple full and steadily working his way up.

So I was shocked when the doctors told me one day that they were going to put John on a feeding tube.

"He's just not eating," the doctor said.

"What do you mean he's not eating?" I said. "He eats."

"He only eats for you," she told me. "None of the nurses can feed him."

Well, I am half Italian. And you don't tell an Italian mother you are not going to eat.

But I doubt John's willingness to take a bottle from me had anything to do with ethnicity. Nor did it have to do with biology. I did not carry and give birth to this child. But I knew, better than I know that the grass is green, that God had given him to me. And John somehow knew it too. How he knew it remains a mystery to me to this day, but it tells the story of every mother. The mystery of motherhood is that our lives sustain theirs. Physically, emotionally and spiritually.

The feeding tube ended up failing miserably. John stopped breathing when doctors inserted it. They removed it, resuscitated him and sent him home with the one person who could feed him, even though eating from a bottle is normally a prerequisite for leaving the neonatal intensive care unit.

John is now six years old and the best eater in the house. (And that's saying something, believe me.) I might have been put on this earth specifically so I could feed this child. Giving a bottle to a baby sounds simple, inconsequential and even mundane to the important people trying to change the world by enlightening the rest of us about what a meaningful life truly is. But if God ordained I exist to give even just an ounce of nourishment to one of his beloved, I wouldn't dream of asking anything more.

So let the pundits debate the value of motherhood. Let the feminists decry it as a lesser calling — inferior to changing the world through politics or science or art. The world will never fully understand the mystery of motherhood. And that's OK. To tell the truth, I don't either. I just know that there is at least one person on this earth whose life was sustained by my love. And I can't think of a higher calling than that.

–Sherry Boas

ABOUT THE AUTHOR

Sherry Boas spent ten years as a reporter for a daily newspaper, winning numerous awards for her writing. But it is motherhood that has best prepared her for an author's career, as she finds inspiration in the struggles and triumphs of everyday family life.

The Boas family has stood in awed witness to a number of miracles, not the least of which saved the life of their fourth child, who was born at twenty-five weeks gestation, a foot long and a pound and a half, facing a multitude of medical difficulties.

Sherry made her novelist's debut in 2011 with a series of captivating characters whose lives are unpredictably transformed by a woman with Down syndrome. Beloved by readers and critics alike, *Until Lily, Wherever Lily Goes, Life Entwined with Lily's* and *The Things Lily Knew* were inspired by Boas' adopted daughter, who has Down syndrome. The fifth in the series, *Things Unknown to Lily,* is slated for release in spring 2015. Boas is also author of a number of children's books, including *Victoria's Sparrows, Little Maximus Myers* and *Billowtail.*

Sherry welcomes feedback from readers and can be reached at Sherry@LilyTrilogy.com or online at www.CaritasPress.org.

WING TIP
by Sherry Boas

Dante De Luz's steel was forged in his youth, in the crucible of harsh losses and triumphant love. But that steel gets tested like never before as the revelation of a family secret presents the young Catholic priest with the toughest challenge of his life, with stakes that couldn't get any higher.

ROSARY TITLES AVAILABLE FROM
CARITAS PRESS / CATHOLIC WORD

A Mother's Bouquet
Rosary Meditations for Moms

A Father's Heart
Rosary Meditations for Dads

A Child's Treasure
Rosary Meditations for Children

Amazing Love
Rosary Meditations for Teens

Generations of Love
Rosary Meditations for Grandparents

A Servant's Heart
Rosary Meditations for Altar Servers

El Amor de una Madre
(Rosary Meditations for Moms in Spanish)

www.LilyTrilogy.com

www.CaritasPress.org

Caritas Press

(602) 920-2846

Sherry@LilyTrilogy.com